Christian
Playfulness

recreation in the spiritual life

redemptorist
publications

Published by Redemptorist Publications
Wolf's Lane, Chawton, Hampshire, GU34 3HQ, UK
Tel. +44 (0)1420 88222, Fax. +44 (0)1420 88805
Email rp@rpbooks.co.uk, www.rpbooks.co.uk

A registered charity limited by guarantee
Registered in England 03261721

Copyright © Redemptorist Publications 2020
First published January 2020

Edited by Caroline Hodgson
Designed by Emma Repetti

ISBN 978-0-85231-564-4

A CIP catalogue record for this book is available from the British Library.

The publisher gratefully acknowledges permission to use the following copyright material:

Excerpts from the New Revised Standard Version of the Bible: Anglicised Edition, © 1989, 1995, Division of Christian Education of the National Council of the Churches of Christ in the United States of America. Used by permission. All rights reserved.

Printed and bound by School Lane Colour Press Limited

recreation in the spiritual life

Christian
Playfulness

Fr Peter Morris C.Ss.R.

Acknowledgements

I'd like to take the opportunity to thank all those who have supported me in bringing this little piece to print. My novice master, Fr Gary Lauenstein C.Ss.R., who unwittingly sowed the seed for this endeavour back in the early stages of my Redemptorist training. Fr Jim McManus C.Ss.R., who from the beginning has encouraged and inspired me to write. I'm grateful to all those who have responded so positively to the material when it was presented in part during parish missions and other events. I'd like to especially thank my editor, Caroline Hodgson, whose enthusiasm for the project was infectious and whose keen eyes helped to pierce the mists of my earlier unclear moments and enabled the text to flow more smoothly. Finally, I wish to thank all my family, friends and confrères, who have taught me to laugh at myself along the way!

Contents

When picking up a booklet like this, it may be tempting to devour it in one sitting. That is possible but I would try to dissuade you from this. My hope is that you can use this text as a springboard to reflection, prayer and, God-willing, conversion of life. With that in mind, I have provided questions at the end of each chapter for reflection if you are reading this on your own. Those questions will also be useful if you are planning to use this text with a group. They are there only for those who need a little prompting in this process. Some may find other points in the main body of the text that need further thought and prayer.

I have included an appendix for those who will use this book for group work. You may wish to turn to the back and read this before proceeding.

However you use this text, I would ultimately hope that you enjoy reading it as much as I have enjoyed writing and presenting some of the material you will find here. Those who know me well will be able to see my smile creeping in at certain points and I hope you are able to laugh with me along the way.

Introduction

I grew up in a pious household. We prayed together regularly. We went to Mass on Sundays and, given the chance, at other opportunities in between. We went to confession once a fortnight and once or twice a year would stay for a little while at Pluscarden Abbey, a Benedictine monastery in the north of Scotland. We were serious about our faith.

Thankfully, that same family has a great sense of fun. We played games together, and enjoyed dressing up and performing for each other. We could let ourselves go and allow our silliness to shine: we laughed and giggled until we were sore in the sides. We were (and still are) notorious for being the first up on the dance floor at a party or other function (often before any drink has been taken).

When I was going through a protracted conversion experience that led me to consider my vocation to the priesthood, I was in grave danger of thinking that this wonderful part of me – one of the great gifts my family had instilled in my very being – needed to be left behind or hidden.

Fortunately, I had some further experiences that would put a stop to that notion.

One was in my final year at university, when I was in the process of applying for seminary for the diocese. One of the local priests turned up in the chaplaincy one day and we shared a quip and a chuckle or two. Fr Bill Anderson, of happy memory, smiled wickedly, his owlish eyebrows tickling his specs: "I'd heard there was a potential seminarian hanging around here and I must say I was at first slightly wary," he shared conspiratorially, "but I'm so pleased that you're not too serious!" Perhaps he was expecting a bland, boorish chap, dressed in a fashion suited to a man four times his age.

Another was the fact that, during my novitiate year with the Redemptorists in Canada, we would meet each Friday evening after dinner and play board games and card games. I really looked forward to those evenings, even though I suspected it was just another way for our superiors to observe and assess our suitability to carry on with the training.

Should one be scandalised by this? Surely the Christian life, in general, and particularly that of the priesthood, is all about prayer, the sacraments and service of others, with no room for such frivolity? Interestingly, as the editing process of this book proceeded, similar questions were being asked surrounding the installation of the helter skelter in Norwich Cathedral.

In this little booklet, I hope to give my answer. It is written with the sincere hope of encouraging you to allow something which is essential to have its proper place in your life too. In chapter one, I hope to challenge the notion that the ideal Christian has no room for play and dance. In order to build on that, I take a look at the humanity of Jesus in chapter two. Chapter three will hopefully convince you that an excessive focus on work is not only unhealthy but also a vice. In the final chapter I set out a Christian vision of playfulness as part of God's redemptive plan of liberation. The music has started, the people are filling the floor. Take my hand. Allow me to lead you.

Lighten up!

I have sometimes come away from Christian events feeling a little deflated. This is not because I disagreed with what was said, but more often than not as a result of seeing what was under the surface of the message. This hidden message appears to be that a true Christian is very serious – all the time.

I come from a Catholic background, and I can understand this. We are surrounded by images of saints – usually unsmiling. We read the stories of their lives and take in the values of offering things up, constant prayer, and giving one's whole life to God and the service of God's people. We absorb messages from hymns, like "Sweet Sacrament Divine", in which we are encouraged to pray intimately with Jesus, telling "our tale of misery". We are specialists in gloom and penance!

Pope Francis has attempted to shake up this perception. I loved it when I read him saying: "An evangeliser must never look like someone who has just come back from a funeral!"[1] Elsewhere he reminded the Church that, "Far from being timid, morose, acerbic or melancholy, or putting on a dreary face, the saints are joyful and full of good humour".[2] The fact that all three titles of his Apostolic Exhortations to date refer to "joy" shows that he is attempting to convey a message to the Christian world – that joy is a mark of the true Christian believer.

I am not suggesting that Christians must become frivolous jesters – *that* has the potential to be harmful in certain circumstances. There is a time for everything – appropriate solemnity and sensitivity are vital for living with each other, especially in times of sorrow. Yet a Spirit-filled existence would surely include a certain amount of light-heartedness. G.K. Chesterton, in his characteristically witty way, argued:

> Modern investigators of miraculous history have solemnly admitted that a characteristic of the great saints is their power of "levitation". They might go further; a characteristic of the great saints is their power of levity. Angels can fly because they can take themselves lightly… Pride is the downward drag of all things into an easy solemnity… Seriousness is not a virtue… It is really a natural trend or lapse into taking one's self gravely, because it is the easiest thing to do… It is easy to be heavy: hard to be light. Satan fell by the force of gravity.[4]

In my opinion, Chesterton hit the nail on the head: Christians are called to tread the narrow path of levity, inspired by the saints, who rose above the easy road of being overly grave. Living lightly is holy.

In his great chapter on play in the second volume of his *Free and Faithful in Christ*, the Redemptorist moral theologian Fr Bernard Häring C.Ss.R. wrote:

> Whoever knows how to play and to dance can take things seriously. He is interested in what he is doing, yet his seriousness is serenity, joy, overflowing liberty. In play we learn the kind of seriousness which is completely human and so far away from the sad seriousness of those who see life only as a burden and not as a gift.[5]

When we take part in something recreational – be it a game, dancing, art or music, it is still important to understand the rules, technique and so on. Yet part of the joy that comes from recreation is knowing that there won't be serious consequences if we don't get it a hundred per cent right. We discover freedom. We discover a new side of ourselves that is often not expressed in our work. We find that we can be creative, spontaneous, or simply let our hair down.

The fact that these activities are not compulsory, but we take part in them anyway, expresses something of God. God created many things in the world, even us, which God did not need to make, but did. These things just are. This tells us that there is something playful about God. The Jesuit philosopher Fr James Schall SJ, suggested that:

> We take the world too seriously, too grimly. If we do not believe in God, we must believe in the supreme importance of the world. And the world cannot bear such seriousness. It makes such a small faith. The existence of God frees us from the solemnity of the world.[6]

Creatures throughout the world range from the majestic and magnificent to the ridiculously bizarre and, frankly, funny. I can't look at nature closely without suspecting that God has a fantastic sense of humour and bundles of playfulness. With that in mind, I can easily picture God having a chuckle when I get all serious about things.

For instance, when fully flowered the *Ophrys apifera*, known as the bee orchid, mimics the shape of a female bee. This attracts male bees, who have their wicked way with these flowers and buzz off. The poor boys have been duped and, in the process, help to pollinate the beautiful flower.

We ourselves begotten and born like the other beasts, we who then become children and move forward from youth to the wrinkles of old age, we who are like flowers which last but for a moment and who then die and are transported into that other life – truly we deserve to be looked upon as a children's game played by God.

St Maximus the Confessor[7]

"But Father!" I hear you protest, "where in the Bible does it say anything about God being playful?" In answer, for a start we need look no further than the book of Proverbs, where the figure of the Wisdom of God is presented as playful:

> When he established the heavens, I was there… when he marked out the foundations of the earth, then I was beside him, like a master worker; and I was daily his delight, rejoicing before him always, rejoicing in his inhabited world and delighting in the human race. (Proverbs 8:27. 29-31)

It's interesting to note that the phrase translated here as "master worker" can also be given as "little child". Häring also replaces the phrase "rejoicing" with "playing".[8] Sometimes it's good to be aware that our scriptural passages may contain double meanings that we would not otherwise be aware of, because we may not know the original language. There is a richness in the writing that can bring fresh perspectives to our lives. The image of a child playing before God and the idea that God delights in this playfulness surely encourages us to see playfulness as part of the Christian life.

When I was growing up, there were times when our parish community would get together for social evenings. Memorable moments for me include the traditional Scottish social dancing that, thankfully, we had learned at school. My brother and I used to jokingly complain about the talon-like grip of some of the elderly ladies during such dances. Those were moments of joy and community bonding. Yet not everyone would see it that way.

It is rather unfortunate that within Christian history there has been a great suspicion of dance. In one of his sermons, St John Chrysostom said, "where there is dancing there is the devil".[9] This may be understandable, given that some kinds of dancing, such as pole dancing, are overtly sexual, provocative or inappropriate. Yet to shun dance in all situations may be taking things too far. I find a good contrast to Chrysostom in St Gregory Nazianzen, who preached with a little more balance (and, dare I say it, reference to scripture):

> But if you dance, because you are a lover of feasts and festivities, then you may; but do not dance the dance of the shameless Herodias who brought death to the Baptist. No; dance the dance of David before the ark of God, for I believe that such a dance is the mystery of sweet motion and nimble gesture of one who walks before God.[10]

Dancing can give glory to God or can play against us or others. It is not a black-and-white issue. Häring, again, commenting on the tendency of Christian theologians to be suspicious of the arts, made this point well when he wrote:

> [In] the long run, theology did a great disservice to human culture and human health when its approach remained negative, bedevilling all that is play, theatre. We cannot redeem the world by rigorism. Only through a positive appreciation and clear understanding of the significance of good play can we contribute to the promotion of culture.[11]

What Häring was trying to say is that redemption does not come from uncompromising strictness ("rigorism"). Yes, discipline is a good thing. Yet if our theology tells us there's nothing good out there that Christians can be involved in, it sounds like condemning those things which are good in God's creation. This attitude sounds sinful to me, even heretical. We would do well to recognise what is good for us in the world.

The saying goes: "The devil makes work for idle hands." It's an attitude which has led to many people developing an unhealthy work ethic, with frantically busy work lives that leave little room for recreation. Christians are by no means immune to this. Furthermore, the way in which Jesus' parable of the unjust judge (Luke 18:1-8) and St Paul's encouragement to "persevere in prayer" (Romans 12:12), are sometimes interpreted, has created a faith focused on endurance and persistence, overly intense Christians and a Church that often forgets that it's not only okay, but important, to let one's hair down now and again. With this in mind, we shall proceed to reflect on the person of Jesus.

> This loving conversation does not demand that you constantly strain your mind at the expense of your other activities or even your recreation. It only requires that, without neglecting your other obligations, you act on occasion toward God in the same way that you act toward those whom you love or who love you.
>
> St Alphonsus Liguori (Doctor of the Church)[12]

Questions for reflection or discussion

- Do I believe that being a good Christian involves being serious all the time? Are there examples of Christian people from my past that may have fostered this idea?

- What other sides of myself can I discover in recreation? Do I like these sides of myself?

- How do I view other people when I'm playing with them?

- Is there something in my background that makes me view dancing as good or bad?

- Have I ever had any bad experiences in a recreational environment? How has this affected my current views of recreational activities?

- What difference does my belief in God make to how I see the world?

Jesus is human

Once, when I was abroad with my Redemptorist student community, I remember eating out one evening. As so often, there was a TV on in the background. It's always distracting, but on this occasion I found it frustrating as well. The programme being shown was a film of the life of Jesus. I couldn't understand what was being said, but I could tell that the actor playing Jesus was, bluntly, playing him as boring. He was speaking in monotone and his facial expression did not look kind at all.

That was not the only time that a film about Jesus has disappointed me. The same goes for some of the images out there. Jesus is often portrayed so seriously – forever glum, with almost no hint of personality or humour. Does this not strike you as odd? I'm not suggesting that Jesus should be played by Jim Carrey or John Cleese (entertaining as that may be), but I think there's something missing. In his years of public ministry, Jesus was at times mobbed by people. There was something attractive about this man. They wanted to spend time with him. The fact that fairly recent images of Jesus smiling or laughing are so unpopular show us that we have culturally accepted a humourless version of Christ.

I don't know about you, but if I spent a considerable amount of time with someone and all they did was teach me all kinds of moral lessons, I'd give up on that friendship pretty quickly. But it's as though this is exactly what we have reduced Jesus to in our popular imagination. In some sense, we have not fully recognised Jesus' humanity.

Since the Ecumenical Councils of the early centuries the Christian Church has professed a faith that Jesus is fully divine and fully human. There will be times when one may be stressed over the other, however neither can be denied if we are to remain faithful to orthodoxy.

> The Logos on high plays, stirring the whole cosmos back and forth,
>
> as he wills, into shapes of every kind.
>
> St Gregory Nazianzen (Doctor of the Church)[13]

The Second Vatican Council teaches that Christ "fully reveals humanity to themselves and brings to light their most high calling."[14] For this reason, we are to look to him for what it means for us to be fully human, to live a full life.

Jesus came from a small village in first-century Palestine which had a strong family ethos, and he was highly likely to have attended several weddings.

It is not surprising, then, that in some of his parables Jesus uses the image of a wedding to preach about the kingdom of God. A wedding was a moment in a family's life when ordinary work would stop and people would feast. In contrast to modern-day western culture, a wedding would last several days. José Pagola described this well:

> A wedding was a spirited family and community festival. The very best. Friends and family members accompanied the young couple for several days, eating and drinking with them, performing

wedding dances and singing love songs… [Jesus] apparently loved being with the couples during these festive days, eating, singing and dancing with them.[15]

> "Look, he comes, leaping upon the mountains, bounding over the hills. My beloved is like a gazelle or a young stag" (Song of Songs 2:8-9). What is meant by this "leaping"? The Logos [Word] leapt from heaven into the womb of the Virgin, he leapt from the womb of his mother on to the cross, from the cross into Hades and from Hades once more back to the earth – O the new resurrection! And he leapt from the earth into heaven where he sits on the right hand of the Father. And he will again leap on to the earth with glory to bring judgement.
>
> Hippolytus of Rome[16]

Fr Gerard Hughes SJ, in his classic spiritual book, *God of Surprises*, writes about a retreatant he refers to as Fred who, as part of an exercise in Ignatian contemplation, prayed about the wedding at Cana:

> He had a vivid imagination and had seen tables heaped with food set out beneath a blue sky. The guests were dancing and it was a scene of great merriment. "Did you see Christ?" I asked. "Yes," he said, "Christ was sitting upright on a straight-backed chair, clothed in a white robe, a staff in his hand, a crown of thorns on his head, looking disapproving.[17]

It doesn't help that most of the images depicting the wedding at Cana are not far off Fred's idea. People might even think of Jesus as a Pioneer,[18] reluctantly changing water into wine at Mary's request before retreating to the corner with his lemonade, rolling his eyes while watching the others enjoy the wine that he's just provided. "Mother, don't look at me like that, *you* were the one who made me do it in the first place!"

Let us not forget Jesus' response to hearing his critics:

> John the Baptist has come eating no bread and drinking no wine, and you say, "He has a demon"; the Son of Man has come eating and drinking, and you say, "Look, a glutton and a drunkard, a friend of tax collectors and sinners!" (Luke 7:33-34)

In this case Jesus was trying to tell his hearers, in jumping to the conclusion that he must be drunk because he was drinking wine, that they were putting two and two together and getting eight! Their conclusions were way off the mark. Yet I think it's safe to say that Jesus must have been seen partaking in such festivities to draw peoples' attention to his drinking wine. As the saying goes, "There's no smoke without fire." Let me make it clear that I am not suggesting that Jesus got drunk at such occasions. Just that he was free and healthy enough to be part of it.

Furthermore, given that Jesus uses the image of a wedding feast for the kingdom of God, it would be odd for him to be suspicious of festivity and everything associated with it, including dancing and singing! As Fr Timothy Radcliffe OP has suggested, "The first preaching of the gospel is the festivity of Jesus – eating, drinking and taking pleasure in the company of just about anyone."[19]

It seems to me that if we spend just a little time digging into the scriptural texts, the overly-serious, party-pooper Jesus we think we have come to know and revere begins to turn into someone much more attractive – a jovial, humorous character who embraces life in all its wonder and beauty. If I were to come into our faith for the first time, this is the kind of person I could imagine spending time with, who I could come to know and love deeply. I cannot recommend enough to the reader picking up the book by Fr James Martin SJ, *Between Heaven and Mirth*, which opened my eyes to see the Christ who jokes and banters with his hearers:

> When I imagine Jesus, it is not simply as a person who heals the sick, raises the dead, stills the storm, and preaches the good news. It's also as a man of great goodwill and compassion, with a zest for life, someone unafraid of controversy, free to be who he knows himself to be, and brimming with generous good humour. Full of high spirits. Playful. Even fun.[20]

Questions for reflection or discussion

- Am I comfortable with the notion that Jesus is fully human? If not, why not?

- In my prayer life, do I ever joke with Jesus? Would I ever bring myself to imagine him laughing with me about my own foibles?

- How have images of Jesus influenced my understanding of his personality?

- If I saw Jesus dancing and drinking wine at a party, how would I react?

Spotlight on the saints – John Bradburne

John Bradburne was a lay Englishman who cared for lepers in what was then Rhodesia, now Zimbabwe. He is a candidate for canonisation. The following is from my confrère, Fr George Webster C.Ss.R.:

"What impressed me most about John was his joyousness. He loved life! And not just in a sentimental way. He was so grateful for it! I remember him rejoicing in something as simple as a person's walk – he described someone running with the flowing ease of an antelope. His religion wasn't in terms of pious acts but more about opening one's eyes wide enough to see beauty as a reflection of God: the beauty of the jaws of a dog, a speckled snake, a child's face. He would make witty comments as we drove to the cinema, he would be like a child next to me wondering at the simple things around us. He enjoyed a drink with friends. In the main, the man was the message. He gave us hope in a suffering world, for which he sincerely mourned. For instance, when we were attending the funeral of one of his best friends, who was shot by government forces, he was so serene when others were full of condemnation and anger. He embodied the value that life could be admired and appreciated because it is a gift from God."

All work and no play

One day my family asked me why I was walking so fast. They were visiting me for a long weekend during my time of study in London. I had unwittingly taken on a new pace – that of the rat race – and I was keeping it up when I was supposed to be relaxed and enjoying their company. My mad dash mainly happened on the London Underground: running up and down escalators, threading through crowds to catch a train. But even when I was above ground I was sprinting across streets to get to my destination as quickly as possible.

I didn't realise how crazy it was until the people who knew me best pointed it out. I was leading them around as if we were in a Benny Hill sketch. The only thing missing was the silly background music. I had bought into a system that kept my heart racing, and my mind and body moving from one thing to the next with no opportunity to rest, no time to stop and smell the roses.

The fact that society, with our work ethic, appears to endorse this kind of behaviour seems to me to be a very serious problem. Bryan Robinson, in his "guidebook" on workaholism, *Chained to the Desk*, summed this up well when he wrote:

> If you tell people they are a workaholic, they usually chuckle. The label is tossed around with abandon in social gatherings, not as a problem but a badge of honor. Corporate climbers wear the workaholic name with pride, proclaiming their loyalty on behalf

of the company, announcing that they binged for eighteen hours or three days on a project as something of which to be proud. But rarely do you hear adults boasting about a three-day drunk or proclaim that they binged on an entire apple pie.[21]

It seems that workaholism is the socially acceptable addiction – even though society is, in one way or another, in denial that it is one. Diane Fassel, in her book, *Working Ourselves to Death*, refers to it as "the 'cleanest' of all the addictions."[22]

One of the effects of this addiction is that the individual's time is so swallowed up in their work that they have little – or even no – time for family or community. Pope Francis, in "The Joy of Love", pointed out:

> In our day, the problem no longer seems to be the overbearing presence of the father so much as his absence, his not being there. Fathers are so caught up in themselves and their work, and at times in their own self-fulfilment, that they neglect their families.[23]

It is probably good to point out that not all workaholics are male or fathers. Yes, the workaholic would rationalise that they are benefiting their children with the comforts of financial support that working so much brings. Yet in doing so they run the risk of depriving their children of something humanly vital – a solid, supportive relationship with a parental figure.

I also frequently come across mothers who appear to be so wrapped up in all the activities of running family life smoothly that they seem not to have a moment to themselves. Recreation disappears from their lives when they start a family. They feel so guilty for taking some moments away to be with friends.

Getting someone in to babysit is almost like admitting defeat in the task of being a good mother. The pressure to be the perfect mother takes its toll on their mental health – resentment and depression lurk around the corner.

On seeing the misery and destructiveness of this state of things, I can imagine the devil rubbing his hands with delight. This has his fingerprints all over it. To help explain this, I look to the psychologist, Rollo May, who wrote:

> Satan, or the devil, comes from the Greek word, *diabolos*, "diabolic" is the term in contemporary English. *Diabolos*, interestingly enough, literally means "to tear apart" (*dia-bollein*). Now it is fascinating to note that this diabolic is the antonym [opposite] to "symbolic." The latter comes from *symbollein*, and means "to throw together," to unite… The *symbolic* is that which draws together, ties, integrates the individual in himself and with his group; the *diabolic*, in contrast, is that which disintegrates and tears apart.[24]

Addictions not only break down an individual within themselves but also pull apart our relationships and society in general. The good news is that we have a God who wishes to clothe us with integrity, that is, wholeness.

Though some may not identify themselves as workaholics, they may relate with the frantic pursuit of activity, of keeping busy. Often when asked how things are going, people will respond, "I'm keeping busy." The Benedictine spiritual writer, Fr Christopher Jamison OSB, identified this tendency as a sign of pride. He defined this sin – that felled Satan – in his book, *Finding Happiness*, as maintaining "self-importance". Keeping busy is a way of showing ourselves that we are the real linchpins of our little world, which leaves God out of the picture or, at best, pushes God to the side. Jamison suggests the antidote to pride is:

Wasting time creatively, such as playing with our children or by giving time to those who at the material level give nothing back, such as visiting the sick or the lonely... We know that such "wasted time" makes us happier than any amount of "being busy". The reason is that these are acts of loving kindness that come from a pure heart.[25]

It may be a good idea to ask ourselves if our work or our busyness contributes to our sense of dignity as a human person. In his encyclical on human work, Pope St John Paul II expressed the goodness of work in this way:

It is not only good in the sense that it is useful or something to enjoy; it is also good as being something worthy, that is to say, something that corresponds to man's dignity, that expresses this dignity and increases it.[26]

There is something wrong going on if, by our work or busy lifestyle, our human life becomes stunted in some way.[27] We are robbing ourselves, or perhaps we are being robbed, of our humanity. Yes, work is supposed to give us a sense of dignity and the knowledge that we are contributing positively in some way to society at large. Yet when work becomes the end in itself – when it has us in its vice – our freedom has been diminished.

An aspect of being human is having a life apart from our work. If this gets diminished we lose parts of our identity and become very one-sided and bland. The wonderful thing about play is that it brings out another part of ourselves that does not necessarily see the light of day elsewhere. It can often bring out our joy, or mirth, as some put it.

Playfulness acts against boredom. And being boring is not the greatest witness to others. St Thomas Aquinas went as far to say that there is something sinful in boring our neighbour or in not bringing pleasure to others. Aquinas suggested that:

Now a man who is without mirth, not only is lacking in playful speech, but is also burdensome to others, since he is deaf to the moderate mirth of others... Consequently they are vicious, and are said to be boorish or rude.[28]

Our lack of playfulness can have a negative effect on others. In my time hearing confessions since being ordained priest, I have never heard anyone say, "Bless me, Father, I have sinned... I bored my wife to tears talking about football the other day."

Spotlight on the saints – St Philip Neri

And what Philip taught by words, he was pitiless in inculcating both in himself and in others who sought direction from him, thereby developing an unbelievable talent for humour and a wealth of practical jokes... He would be seen going through the streets with a bunch of broom flowers in his hand, stopping every few steps to sniff it with an expression of ecstasy, as if he were smelling the most aromatic of flowers. Or he would go about solemnly while wearing a cushion on his head like a turban, or wearing a coat made of foxtails, which he would then give to one of his companions to keep him warm – this in the middle of summer![29]

When we neglect our social lives, especially when we allow friendships to fade from our list of priorities, we can become more and more irritable. It can be so tempting to pursue good causes with such enthusiasm that other parts of our lives take second place. What happens in the process is that we can descend into anger and bitterness. As Fr Ronald Rolheiser OMI suggested, especially if we are fighting for the cause of justice, which can be incredibly lonely work:

> It is all too easy to get angry, to feel self-righteous, to fill with bitterness, to become selective in our prophecy and to hate the very people we are trying to save.[30]

This will only taint our work and even our prayer lives. According to Rolheiser:

> Only friendship can save us. Loving, challenging friends who can melt our bitterness and free us from the need to be angry are as critical within the spiritual life as are prayer and social justice. To neglect friendship is to court bitterness and perversion.[31]

Someone who is boring, who has allowed their work to take over, to overly deplete their energy, who has become angry and bitter, is not an attractive person at all. Moreover, I would argue that they would not be an adequate witness to the good news of Jesus. As Pope Francis wrote, the Church grows "by attraction".[32] Good evangelists are attractive to others in their lifestyle and way of being.

Questions for reflection or discussion

- Do I work too much? Does my work consume my time to the point that I have no other activities in my life as a respite from it?

- What do I do to relax? Is it a healthy pursuit?

- As a worshipping community or parish, do we have moments for fun or recreation?

- Have I ever been a source of boredom to others?

Glorify the Lord by your lives

At some stage in my time as a Redemptorist student in London, I became keenly aware of my need to develop friendships and have healthy recreational pursuits. Thankfully, I was encouraged to do this. I started attending a board gaming club which ran at various locations most days of the week – usually in bars. I continued to go after I was ordained and would still meet new people through it. It was common for people to be surprised by my response to the question: "So, what do you do for a living?" They would look briefly at the pint of beer sitting next to me and say, "But surely priests are not allowed to drink?" I would brush off the question by asking if they had ever seen *Father Ted*! Someone else even asked whether I was really allowed to be at "something like this". I just said that I was sure that if I really wanted to rebel there would be far more imaginative options than sneaking off to play board games!

What saddened me about the reactions of the people I met was that they perceived Christianity only in terms of what Christians are supposedly not allowed to do. Yes, self-denial is a Christian virtue, and Christians are called to be wise and sensible about what

they become involved in. However, as I wrote earlier, it is not truly Christian to write off everything we come across out there as evil. Certainly, since the Second Vatican Council, the Catholic Church is invited to turn towards the world with a positive vision. The Council Fathers taught that "nothing that is genuinely human fails to find an echo in [Christian] hearts".[33] The world is to be seen as:

> The theatre of human history, bearing the marks of its travail, its triumphs and failures, the world, which in the Christian vision has been created and sustained by the love of its maker, which has been freed from the slavery of sin by Christ, who was crucified and rose again in order to break the stranglehold of the evil one so that it might be fashioned anew according to God's design and brought to its fulfilment.[34]

This is a calling to understand how good creation is and to see that Christ has come to restore all creation back to its original intention – to reflect the love of the Father and to glory in this.

The good news of Jesus is a proclamation of the kingdom of God breaking into this world. Jesus proclaimed that this kingdom, though not of this world, was somehow already upon us. Jesus' message, his purpose in coming into the world, is "that they may have life, and have it abundantly" (John 10:10). There's an exuberance there, a generosity. As one of my confrères, Fr Thomas MacCarte C.Ss.R., preaches, the redemption that Jesus has come to bring is not a mean redemption, limited in small portions like the sachets we dispense sugar or sauce from, but something overwhelmingly generous. We get more than we bargain for with Jesus.

Jesus lived his life showing us this great truth of the generosity of God. This abundance was shown in the mystery of the wedding at Cana. Jesus' miracle of turning water into wine was not just "Wow, he can do this!" It has a deeper meaning in the sheer abundance that can be found in God. Pope Benedict XVI explained this well when he wrote:

> The sign of God is overflowing generosity. We see it in the multiplication of the loaves; we see it again and again – most of all, though, at the centre of salvation history, in the fact that he lavishly spends himself for the lowly creature, man. This abundant giving is his "glory". The superabundance of Cana is therefore a sign that God's feast with humanity, his self-giving for men, has begun.[35]

The sheer amount of wine that Jesus produced at the wedding was far more than was necessary for the occasion. In that moment, Jesus showed he has no interest in rations. To this I would like to add what Fr James Martin said, having made some very interesting points about the saints who came to know and live with this joy: "I bet that the man whose first miracle was to turn water into wine at the wedding feast of Cana understood the need to have some high spirits in life."[36]

Spotlight on the saints – Blessed Francis Xavier Seelos C.Ss.R.

Father Joseph Firle said that all who came to [Seelos] were attracted by his merry manner; his joyful disposition accompanied by a calm serenity inspired all with great reverence and esteem.[37]

"Once a Father arrived in Pittsburgh and seemed perplexed when he noticed that his saliva was black the next morning. Seelos, who knew this was caused by Pittsburgh's smoky atmosphere, sidled up to him and said, 'What's the matter? Are you suffering from some internal disease?' All the Fathers chuckled. His constant attitude of geniality made all who knew him realize that he was a man who truly wished them well.[38]

But besides his piety and profound erudition, he had an abundance of jokes and liked to tell them. When he told a joke, he would look at the person to whom he was telling it and laugh with such cordiality and hilarity that he was like a boy."[39]

My response to this Gospel cannot be anything but joy! As Pope Paul VI wrote, "no one is excluded from the joy brought by the Lord."[40] This joy is for you and me, here and now. In this life we can participate in this deep joy in good, healthy play, without guilt or fear. When we play, we can tap into this joy. Fr Bernard Häring C.Ss.R. explains that:

There is a special exhilaration in play as interplay, as an expression of partnership and shared joy. This is a paradigm of all of God's works. Creation and incarnation, and the whole history of salvation are expression and revelation of God's free creative and redemptive love. Our whole existence is "at home" if we know that we are in the hands of God and that his play with us is holy and liberating, the highest manifestation of his love.[41]

It brings me great comfort to know that when I play, I can do so in the knowledge that not only am I in God's hands, but I also reflect God's creative and redemptive love to others.

Jesus has come to set us free. "If you continue in my word, you are truly my disciples; and you will know the truth, and the truth will make you free" (John 8:31-32). In addition it is good to reflect on what can be called Jesus' mission statement, the text he reads out at the beginning of his public ministry from the prophet Isaiah: "He has sent me to proclaim release to the captives" (Luke 4:18; Isaiah 61:1). Jesus has come to liberate us from the prisons that we find ourselves in. To me, such prisons include that of excessive guilt and the domination of work.

> Once there was a time when the whole of rational creation formed a single dancing chorus looking upwards to the one leader of this dance... Our first parents danced in among the angelic powers. But the beginning of sin made an end of the sweet pounds of this chorus... Since then man has been deprived of this communion with the angels, and, since the fall, must sweat and most arduously toil to do battle with and conquer the spirit that, thanks to sin, now weighs upon him; but the spoils of victory will be these: that which was lost in his original defeat will once more be his to enjoy, and once again he will take part in the dancing of the divine chorus.
>
> St Gregory of Nyssa[42]

The liberating power of Jesus remakes us into the fully human person that God wants us to be. The German theologian Cardinal Walter Kasper put it well when he wrote:

> God does not oppress man, but sets his creative forces free. Indebted human existence is realized in play and celebration.

Only where man is not merely *homo faber*, worker, but also *homo ludens*, man at play, can he be described as genuinely human and as a free man who rises above life's immediate needs. Jesus' exhortation, not to be anxious and concerned for our life, but first to seek the kingdom of God and his justice (see Matthew 6:25-33), reveals an essential basic feature of a redeemed human existence.[43]

There are things that we need to do to survive: to work, to eat, to sleep. Yet if we wish to become fully human we need to do things which are not obligatory. To live a life of pure obligation is not a full life at all and not the redeemed existence that Jesus offers us.

I would like to leave you with an extract from C.S. Lewis' classic, *The Screwtape Letters*. For those who are not familiar with this work, Screwtape is a demon writing some advice to another demon, Wormwood, about tempting a particular person away from God, who is referred to as "the Enemy". Being an evil spirit, he abhors anything good:

> Fun is closely related to joy – a sort of emotional froth arising from the play instinct. It is very little use to us. It can sometimes be used, of course, to divert humans from something else which the Enemy would like them to be feeling or doing: but in itself it has wholly undesirable tendencies; it promotes charity, courage, contentment, and many other evils.[44]

Questions for reflection or discussion

- When I recreate, do I feel guilty? Is there something from my past which has led to this feeling? If I do feel guilt, do I think it is from God or from elsewhere?

- When I think of Jesus' mission to liberate me, how do I see this happening? How can I take steps to allow this to happen – to accept the invitation of Jesus to live life in abundance?

- Having read this booklet, what, if anything, are my hopes for the future?

I hope that this little booklet has given you the impression that good recreation has a place in the Christian life. It is not my intention to paint a picture of a hedonistic life, where we end up buying into the consumerist model of society, taking part in what Pope Francis called "the feverish pursuit of frivolous pleasures".[45] Yet my impression, in the short time I have ministered as a priest, is that the average Christian, though they may know within themselves the goodness of balance in their lives, is not aware that there is a theological backing for taking time out here and there.

On the occasions that I conclude the Mass with the words, "Go in peace, glorifying the Lord by your life", I sincerely hope that the people present feel empowered to do just that. I hope that they know that they can give glory to God in all aspects of their lives, and that they can become joyful witnesses to our awesome God.

Working with a group

In this appendix I would like to offer some thoughts on working with groups, to help those who may be using this book with their church, reading or prayer group, or indeed any other kind of group. Some of the points may seem common sense or obvious, although it's helpful to think them through before launching into any games or other activities designed to promote a more playful atmosphere.

How you work with a group will, of course, depend on its particular aim. It may be focused on playfulness, or it may be that people have come together to work with a more serious subject (for example, a Lent course or counselling group). Even so, you may want to begin and/or finish on a lighthearted note. Sometimes you may need to make a snap judgement as to whether or not it's appropriate to lift the mood, depending on what has happened within the group.

Encouraging playfulness

This is potentially the most challenging aspect for a group working with this book. I would struggle to come up with specific proposals for encouraging playfulness. Let me explain. I have been in youth and other church groups where icebreakers have been used. I can sense the unease that people have with these kinds of activities. There is a cringe factor which can make some of us roll our eyes, grin and bear it, or even just leave us feeling utterly uncomfortable. I totally get it.

On the other hand, games can be the catalyst that bonds a group. There's something magical about it, and people can be brought together by laughing at the silliness or shared embarrassment of it all. Lists of suggested icebreakers can be found on plenty of websites, especially for youth work. Of course, not all such activities will be suitable for all groups working with this book, especially those which require some agility.

What kind of playfulness you want to encourage depends very much on you and the group you're working with. There are no hard and fast rules. A good start is to open that question up to the group. Do you like board games? Would you run a mile at the idea of dressing up or putting on a panto, or would it appeal to you? Is everyone in the group comfortable with what you're proposing?

One of my sisters loves to host parties for family and friends, and a frequent feature are silly games to lighten things up. One hilarious example involves knocking tennis balls off upturned disposable cups. The twist is that you have to do it by placing a small orange into the leg of a pair of tights and place them on your head, and attempting to do the deed with the orange. Two players race to knock the balls down, looking like clumsy elephants.

As I mentioned earlier, I am a lover of board games and card games. Thankfully, at the time of writing, they are having something of a renaissance. I particularly enjoy party games that are a subgenre of board games. These tend to be simpler, with fewer rules, enabling everyone to get involved straight away and they can often be played with larger groups. A couple of my favourite party games, which usually lead to a lot of laughter, are "Say Anything" and "Telestrations". I've been particularly sore after laughing so hard playing the latter. For those who don't like the idea of competition, there are some cooperative board games, such as "Pandemic", "Forbidden Island"

and "Robinson Crusoe", where everyone works together to beat the game. There are also a good number of games, known in the gaming community as "fillers", which last fifteen to twenty minutes and are good if there is a time constraint. Whatever it may be, playing a game at the end of a session can be a good way of rounding off.

Above all, a little lightheartedness goes a long way with a group. Even as individuals share their thoughts and feelings, it helps to add a little humour. Of course, some humour can hurt and alienate people, even when it's well-intended. The surest way to keep it safe is that to be self-deprecating – laughing at ourselves. And ultimately it is good to keep in mind the image of Jesus having a good laugh alongside us.

Giving everyone a voice – facilitating group discussion

Spontaneity is at the very heart of playfulness and recreation. Like fun, it cannot be forced, but happens organically. Gardeners know that when they plant seeds or bulbs, they need to make sure that they have the appropriate circumstances – the right soil quality, for instance, enough natural light and sufficient water. In the same way it is possible for a facilitator to provide the ideal environment for spontaneity and playfulness. This means creating a safe, comfortable space, so that everybody feels included and able to participate and contribute fully. If you want to create a space where playfulness can flourish, particularly within an established group, it's important to facilitate good, honest discussion beforehand, to give the group a shared purpose, identify any boundaries, limitations or anxieties, and foster a sense of cooperation. These conversations can, of themselves, be very powerful. So this section offers some suggestions for facilitators who hope to encourage playfulness within a group. Many of these techniques can be carried forward and used in recreation itself.

A classic pitfall in any group work is allowing one or more members of the group to dominate. There are various ways for a leader or facilitator to avoid this. In a discussion, for example, you might try to gently intercept at a convenient moment and, with sensitivity and tact, ask others for their thoughts. To avoid hurt feelings, it's helpful to affirm what has been said, before gently suggesting that it would be good to hear what someone else thinks.

In situations where you find that someone is reticent or not participating, it can be helpful to ask their opinion. But there are other ways of encouraging someone shy to share more. You might, for instance, avoid closed questions that require yes or no answers and allow for more in-depth responses. Similarly, you may find it helpful to ask specific questions, to avoid the person feeling overwhelmed by the scope of what is being asked of them, especially if he or she is socially awkward or anxious. At the risk of sounding as though you're interrogating someone, if their answer is short, you might prompt further by asking why they've given the response that they have.

There may come a time when, in spite of your best efforts to facilitate good discussion and sharing, an issue persists. The next step might be to talk to the individuals concerned outside the group setting. Whether it's an over-talker or a shy person, affirm that their opinions and ideas really matter and that everyone's contributions should be heard and respected.

An extreme but very effective method of encouraging good group sharing is to structure the time allotted for sharing. Practically, this involves someone sitting with a timer (a phone, watch or stopwatch) and indicating when it's time to wrap it up. It has the benefit of reining in anyone who's dominant, and possibly encouraging some discipline in their sharing, while giving the others a fair chance to be heard. The risk is that it could intimidate less confident group members when their turn comes around.

The important thing is that, from the outset, the group agrees that all members should have a fair opportunity to share their thoughts. If at any stage during the process this is not being respected, a gentle reminder of this agreement may be in order, whether in the meeting or discreetly outside.

Creating a safe space

The ultimate aim of this book is to promote playfulness as a way to honest self-exploration, both individually and as a wider community. Of course this won't happen if a group tends simply to agree or disagree on theoretical points, which is what can happen when a group is newly formed. It takes time to build trust. One would hope that the time comes when individuals within a group trust each other enough to move beyond the "safety" of superficiality, that is, talking generally or hypothetically, and begin to explore things more deeply, in other words to share their personal experiences, feelings and practices.

It helps to come to an agreement, at least at the first meeting, about confidentiality. What I mean by this is that everyone agrees that whatever is shared stays within the group and is not shared more widely without express permission.[46] This not only helps to allay any anxieties but also challenges the group to practise the important Christian virtue of discretion.

In addition to discussing confidentiality in early meetings, it might be useful to have a discussion about the use of language, to encourage and enable group members to speak with tact, respect and compassion. Simply telling someone that they're wrong can be incredibly hurtful and even damaging. Even an apparently innocuous discussion can become a heated argument and it is the responsibility of the leader or facilitator calmly to bring an end to it and suggest that it may be best to continue another time.[47] This can take courage and needs to be handled with great care, but it is hugely important to protect the sense of safety within the group.

1 Pope Francis, *Evangelii Gaudium* ("The Joy of the Gospel"), 10.

2 Pope Francis, *Gaudete et Exsultate* ("Rejoice and Be Glad"), 122.

3 James Martin SJ, *Between Heaven and Mirth: why joy, humor, and laughter are at the heart of the spiritual life* (New York: Harper One, 2011), 209.

4 G.K. Chesterton, *Orthodoxy* (London: Fontana, 1967), 119-120.

5 Bernard Häring C.Ss.R., *Free and Faithful in Christ: moral theology for priests and laity,* volume II (Slough: St Paul, 1979), 139.

6 James V. Schall SJ, *The Praise of "Sons of Bitches": on the worship of God by fallen men* (Slough: St Paul, 1978), 130.

7 *Ambigua* (*Patrologia Graeca* 91, 1189D), in Hugo Rahner SJ, *Man at Play: or did you ever practise eutrapelia?* (London: Burns & Oates, 1965), 25.

8 Häring, *Free and Faithful in Christ,* II, 141.

9 John Chrysostom, *Homiliae in Matthaeum,* 48[49], 3, translated by Brian Battershaw & Edward Quinn, in Hugo Rahner SJ, *Man at Play: or did you ever practise eutrapelia?* (London: Burns & Oates, 1965), 76.

10 Gregory Nazianzen, *Orationes,* V, 35, in Rahner, *Man at Play,* 77.

11 Häring, *Free and Faithful in Christ,* II, 143.

12 Alphonsus Liguori, "Conversing with God as a Friend", Frederick M. Jones C.Ss.R. (Ed.), in *Alphonsus Liguori: selected writings* (Mahwah: Paulist, 1999), 273-290, 276.

13 Gregory Nazianzen, *Carmina,* I, 2, 2, vv. 589-590, in Rahner, *Man at Play,* 23.

14 Vatican II, *Gaudium et Spes* ("Pastoral Constitution on the Church in the Modern World"), 22.

15 José Pagola, *Jesus: an historical approximation* (New York: Convivium, 2009), 66.

16 Hippolytus, *In Canticum,* II, in Rahner, *Man at Play,* 77.

17 Gerard Hughes SJ, *God of Surprises* (London: DLT, 1985), 36.

18 The Pioneer Total Abstinence Association is a laudable movement that began in Ireland at the end of the nineteenth century. It is a spiritual response to the damage done to society by alcoholism. Members take a pledge of total abstinence from alcohol for life.

19 Timothy Radcliffe OP, *Why Go To Church? The drama of the Eucharist* (London: Continuum, 2008), 203.

20 Martin, *Between Heaven and Mirth,* 54-55.

21 Bryan Robinson, *Chained to the Desk: a guidebook for workaholics, their partners and children, and the clinicians who treat them,* 3rd edn (NY: New York University Press, 2014), 2.

22 Diane Fassel, *Working Ourselves to Death: the high cost of workaholism and the rewards of recovery* (Lincoln, NE: iUniverse, 2000), vii.

23 Pope Francis, *Amoris Laetitia* ("The Joy of Love"), 176.

24   Rollo May, *Love and Will* (London: Souvenir, 1969), 138.

25   Abbot Christopher Jamison OSB, *Finding Happiness: monastic steps for a fulfilling life* (London: Weidenfeld & Nicolson, 2008), 184.

26   Pope John Paul II, *Laborem Exercens* ("Through Work"), 9.

27   The same, of course, applies when we develop an aversion to work when we would otherwise be healthy enough for it.

28   St Thomas Aquinas, *Summa Theologiae*, II: II, Q.168, art. 4.

29   Paul Türks of the Oratory, *Philip Neri: the fire of joy* (Edinburgh: T&T Clark, 1995), 118.

30   Ronald Rolheiser OMI, *Forgotten Among the Lilies: learning to love beyond our fears* (London: Doubleday, 2005), 34.

31   Rolheiser, *Forgotten Among the Lilies*, 34-35.

32   Pope Francis, *Evangelii Gaudium*, 15.

33   Vatican II, *Gaudium et Spes*, 1.

34   Vatican II, *Gaudium et Spes*, 2.

35   Joseph Ratzinger, *Jesus of Nazareth, Volume I: from the Baptism in the Jordan to the transfiguration*, translated by Adrian J. Walker (London: Bloomsbury, 2007), 252.

36   Martin, *Between Heaven and Mirth*, 118.

37   Michael Curley C.Ss.R., *Cheerful Ascetic: the life of Francis Xavier Seelos* (New Orleans: The Redemptorist Fathers of the New Orleans Vice Province, 1969), 265.

38   Curley, *Cheerful Ascetic*, 265.

39   Curley, *Cheerful Ascetic*, 267.

40   Pope Paul VI, *Gaudete in Domino* ("Rejoice in the Lord"), 22.

41   Häring, *Free and Faithful in Christ,* II, 141.

42   Gregory of Nyssa, *Homiliae in Psalmos,* 6, in Rahner, *Man at Play*, 89-90.

43   Walter Kasper, *Jesus the Christ,* translated by V. Green (London: Burns & Oates, 1976), 214.

44   C.S. Lewis, *The Screwtape Letters* (London: Fount, 1942, 1998), 42.

45   Pope Francis, *Evangelii Gaudium*, 2.

46   There are, of course, exceptions to this, such as disclosures about the abuse of children and vulnerable adults. A group leader or facilitator may have a duty to follow safeguarding procedures and report this kind of information to the police. This needs to be made clear in any discussions about confidentiality.

47   One possibility is to suggest that people write down their feelings about the subject.